Blessed Art Thou

Blessed Art Thou
Mother Lady Mystic Queen

Michael O'Neill McGrath, OSFS
with prayers by
Richard N. Fragomeni

WORLD LIBRARY PUBLICATIONS
Franklin Park, Illinois

Blessed Art Thou © 2004, World Library Publications, the music and liturgy division of J. S. Paluch Company, Inc., 3708 River Road, Suite 400, Franklin Park, Illinois 60131-2158. 800 566-6150 www.wlpmusic.com

All rights reserved under United States copyright law. No part of this book may be reproduced or transmitted in any form or by any means, mechanical, photographic, or electronic, including photocopying, or any information storage or retrieval system, without the written permission of the appropriate copyright owner.

Excerpts from the *New American Bible with Revised New Testament and Psalms* Copyright © 1991, 1986, 1970 Confraternity of Christian Doctrine, Inc., Washington, D.C. Used with permission. All rights reserved. No portion of the *New American Bible* may be reprinted without permission in writing from the copyright holder.

Excerpt from the English translation of *Eucharistic Prayers for Masses of Reconciliation* © 1975, International Committee on English in the Liturgy, Inc. All rights reserved.

Art and commentary by Michael O'Neill McGrath; prayers by Richard N. Fragomeni.

The paintings were done in acrylics on watercolor paper.

This book was edited by Christine Krzystofczyk with assistance from Marcia T. Lucey and Alan J. Hommerding. Design and layout by Christine Enault. Production manager was Deb Johnston. Graphic consultation by Steve Broin. The book was set in San Vito and Berkeley. Printed in South Korea. Graphics TwoFortyFour Inc.

ISBN 1-58459-177-3

To Richard and Liz Caemmerer and Karen Haddon:
artists, pilgrim guides, and dearly loved companions on my journey
to the creative, feminine heart of God

— *M.O.M.*

These prayers in honor of Mary
are dedicated with affection and respect
to Eunice Kennedy Shriver,
who inspires me with her love of the Maid of Nazareth.

— *R.N.F.*

Contents

Preface

Assumption over Bethany

About the paintings

Mother

Mother of God

Cause of Our Joy

Seat of Wisdom

Promised Land of Milk and Honey

Mother of Sorrows

Lady

Our Lady of Peace

Our Lady of Divine Grace, the New Eve

Our Lady of Light

Our Lady of the Rosary

Our Lady of Refuge

Mystic

Virgin of Virgins
Mystical Rose
Dawn of the Mystic Day
Gate of Heaven
Star of the Sea

Queen

Queen of the Apostles
Queen of the Angels
Queen of the Prophets
Queen of the Saints
Queen of the Universe

Preface

My all-time favorite explanation of the Assumption comes from a third-grader in a religion class I once visited. I asked, "Who can tell me what the feast of the Assumption is all about?" hoping for an answer that would perhaps explain it to me, it being one of those mysterious dogma things I've never been able to get my head around. One little boy gave me the response I longed for: "It means that Mary was so holy we just assume she went to heaven." Even as I laughed, I remember thinking the kid was on to something. Out of the mouths of babes and into my permanent memory.

The first scripture reading at Mass on the feast of the Assumption is the familiar one from the book of Revelation about the woman clothed with the sun about to give birth. Beneath her a snarling red dragon lies in wait to devour her baby. These enigmatic symbols and dizzying details seem to have stepped right out of a Bosch painting or a Spielberg film. I've always felt they are not to be taken literally, too wild to be true. Until one day . . .

There I was in the ocean at Bethany Beach, Delaware, minding my own business and riding the rough surf like a baby seal. The rhythm of the pounding water forced knots of tension out of my neck and shoulders, freeing up my head to entertain new ideas for the paintings and writings in this book. Buoyant with joy at all these new bursts of inspiration that were coming at me in waves, I kinda forgot that I'm not much of a swimmer and found myself caught in one of those riptides you learn about on the Discovery Channel. Frantic doggy-paddling only sent me toward France instead of the beach while my desperate leg-stretching to feel the ocean floor caused excruciating cramps.

With stabbing pain in my calf muscles and a mouth full of salty foam, I decided it was time to wave to the lifeguards. One of them leapt from the stand and hit the ground running. I watched her every stride as she raced across the beach, dived into the crashing waves, and tossed me a lifeline. Fished out of the ocean by an eighty-pound college kid, I was filled with gratitude not for the gift of life, but rather that no one on the beach stopped their talking and tanning long enough to gawk at my humiliating drama.

As dramas go, I guess it was pretty anticlimactic. My life never flashed before my eyes and there were no lights or tunnels. I never made any valiant promises to God nor did I have any visions of Mary (or even a minor saint) telling me my work on earth was not yet finished. What I did get in my post-panic calm under the beach umbrella was the inspiration for this painting. I started sketching ideas right then and there in my sketchbook, but never painted anything further until five months later when I was house-bound during a blizzard and feeling anxious about biochemical terrorism. Thus *Assumption over Bethany* was born following a long and occasionally stressful pregnancy.

I imagined Mary hovering above our heads. Some of us on the beach that morning were merely soaking up the sun, sipping lemonade and wondering where to have dinner that evening, while others among us were nearly drowning. Life is like that, isn't it? Birth, death, and the ordinary stuff in between happen at the same time, packing every moment of our day with mystery. We are continually given glimpses not only of God and all that is good and beautiful but of the serpent as well, who lies in wait to devour the baby of the woman so holy we assume she is in heaven watching over us like a lifeguard.

Assumption over Bethany

Salve Regina!
Hail, holy woman,
clothed with the sun,
gracing all creation with
your peaceful radiance,
filling the skies with colorful light.
Amen.

Mater Misericordiae!
Bearer of divine mercy,
enter our chaos with
the serenity of your care,
our distracted world with
the promise of your love.
Set us free from fear.
Show us we are not alone.
Amen.

Spes Nostra, salve!
For you bring us our only hope,
the hope of a world made new,
where all can rest secure,
secure in the good news of your child,
who gives us summertime peace
even in the midst of winter.
Amen.
Alleluia.

About the paintings...

This entire book is about her and for her with prayers both painted and written. Most of the paintings were inspired by titles from the Litany of Loreto, one of the oldest prayers of the Church. The attributes of Mary presented in this litany were frequently derived from the Hebrew Testament that celebrates human love and passion. They have been seen traditionally by the great Christian mystics as metaphors for the love relationship between God and humanity. Two of the titles ("Promised Land" and "Dawn of the Mystic Day") come from the Agathistos, a Greek litany to Mary dating from the sixth century.

The book is divided into four sections to illuminate some recurring themes found in the litanies. These themes mark elements of our own life journeys as well. The titles in the chapter named "Mother" remind us of our hearts' continual longing for nurturing love and the desire to create. These show us the Mary of Bethlehem and Calvary. The images in the section designated "Lady" refer to the gracious Mary who is devoted handmaid and grace-filled servant, the Mary of Nazareth at the Annunciation and Visitation. The "Mystic" group celebrates a more contemplative Mary who exposes us to our own inner potentials and possibilities. She is the Mary of the Presentation, who holds the mysteries of God in her heart. And finally, "Queen" is the title of her ultimate fulfillment as protector of all hearts that long for the love of God. As queen, she is the Mary of Pentecost and the Assumption.

If you have already flipped through this book to look at the pictures, as I hope you have done, you will have seen an array of colors much wider than the blue and white of your grandmother's devotional book. You have caught glimpses of black- and brown-skinned women with the energy of a quiet storm. These images spring from my loving fascination for Black Madonnas, figures carved from single blocks of black wood, which have inspired pilgrims, saints, and sin-sick souls for centuries. They are among the most beloved symbols of spiritual healing and transformation throughout Christian history, and have been empowering for people who bravely struggle to make fresh starts in life.

Just as I have done with the litany titles, I take time-honored tradition and give it my own contemporary twist. It seems impossible to me that we modern Americans could view these venerated symbols of medieval times without being mindful of our own contemporary sensibilities about race and gender. Mary as handmaid, the poor woman who prophetically spoke of being exalted and lifted to high places, takes on richer meaning when seen in the context of African-American and Latin-American history and culture. The Black Madonna, like Guadalupe, enriches our understanding of God's unity and diversity as opposed to the world's divisiveness and intolerance.

I have written commentaries for each of the paintings merely to shed some light on the origins of the colors, shapes, and symbols. Just like the art itself, these commentaries are a mix of the personal and the universal. But, as is always the case when we pray with art, we must remember to give priority to our own stories and experiences of God. In other words, if something I wrote about a painting does not match your own interpretation, then you must let your heart, and not my words, be your guide.

This is exactly how Richard Fragomeni and I chose to collaborate from our very first meeting. He based his prayers on his own experience of the painted images, never wishing to see or know my written commentaries. The prayers he has composed are as beautiful as they are because they come from his own heart and soul, not mine.

I offer heartfelt thanks to Richard for sharing his very rich spiritual gifts with me in this project. He is a poet, mystic, and ideal collaborator! I would also like to thank Mary Prete of World Library Publications, whose enthusiasm and friendship have guided this book along from the beginning; Christine Krzystofczyk, who has so lovingly and patiently tended to details of the entire process; Christine Enault, who took the art and words and designed this exquisite book; Deb Johnston and Steve Broin, who were so helpful in the design process; and Marcia Lucey, copy editor par excellence.

This book is for all of you readers who struggle to find new ways to be faithful in a church and world continually racked by crisis, division, and insecurity. It is for you who maintain an abiding love for Mary, no matter where else you are in your journey with (or from) the church. It is for you who find delight in a God who is more than white and male, whose wholeness and fullness break down our own limits as well. May the colors stimulate you and the words inspire you. And may Mary, who is Mother, Lady, Mystic, and Queen, visit you and find a home in your heart. Blessed is she among women. And blessed, it is safe to assume, are we.

Mother Lady Mystic Queen

Mother of God

. . . Holy Mary,
Mother of God . . .

We say these words so often, dear Lady:
each time we greet you,
each decade of the rosary,
each evening at bedtime,
each morning at prayer.

We say these words so often, dear Mother;
we say them now,
we will say them at the hour
of our death.

We say these words so often, dear Mary;
they lose their sting,
they shock us no more,
they no longer draw us into
the wonder of the Word-made-flesh.

Nevertheless,
still we say them:
. . . Holy Mary,
Mother of God . . .

pray for us seekers
pray for us peacemakers
pray for us poor
pray for us rich
pray for us sick
pray for us lonely
pray for us sinners

that we may do mercy,
O Mother of God;
that we may act justly,
O Mother of God;
that we may walk humbly,
O Mother of God.

Blessed is the fruit of your womb, Jesus
(Hail Mary)

Picture it historically first—a very poor teenage Jewish girl, hardly accounting for anything at all, of less value than a cow in the eyes of many, and living in a land occupied by powerful foreign forces, is visited by an angel who appears one day at her dusty door and makes a momentously strange request: Would she consider having God's baby? After asking some questions and drawing on her knowledge of the prophecies in scripture, she says, "Yes," knowing the risk of being snubbed by her fiancé and, worse, stoned to death by her neighbors and friends. In that incarnational moment of trust and wild abandon, the little girl changes the course of human history.

Now, picture it spiritually. A young woman, not necessarily Jewish, has and holds forever a baby who comes from God and through God and is God, fully human like her, fully divine like his father. Through Mary, our creator puts on a human face and raises the bar of dignity for all of us, especially those of us who are poor, overlooked, and shouldered to the fringes of society because of gender, culture, religion, or sexuality.

Mary, Mother of God, is one of the Creator's greatest gifts. Herself free of fears and sins that routinely ensnare the rest of us, she encourages us in our struggles to be free, urging us on as mothers do, loving us equally in our triumphs and our failures. The Mother of God is the mother of all souls, in love with the baby she consented to bear in a wild moment of abandonment to God. *Fiat* is the first word she teaches us, the word she teaches us again and again.

Cause of Our Joy

Dear God,
thank you for
our joyful sister Mary.

You called her name and
made her a mother.

She said to the angel:
"Let it be done to me!"
She was filled with joy.

You sent her to Elizabeth.
The two cousins exulted
and their babies touched hearts.
They were filled with joy.

The shepherds and the Magi
drew close, summoned by
angels and stars.
And the child,
near his mother,
slept.
All creation was
filled with joy.

Simeon and Anna
greeted the family at last.
Mary presented her child
and fulfilled the law.
With Joseph,
Young and old alike
were filled with joy.

Young Jesus taught the teachers,
dazzled the wise,
troubled his parents,
wakened their wonder and awe.
The world is filled with joy.

Dear God,
thank you for our
joyful sister Mary.
Now we are filled
with joy.

Amen.

Be it done to me according to your word
(Angelus)

St. Francis de Sales once said that when it comes to our relationship with God, we should be like children who run about unafraid of falling when they know their mothers are looking on. It is good for us to recall those days of running, jumping, and leaping through life in the secure trust that God is there to keep us out of harm's way.

It is a holy endeavor to recreate such child-like abandonment, to be so full of joy at just being ourselves.

Remember how it felt to be swung around faster and faster—so fast, in fact, that you couldn't stand up straight when the ride was over, dizzy with excitement on wobbly knees, begging for just one more time?

Such joy is built on trust. We can't enjoy the thrill of spinning out of control if we aren't trustful of the one doing the spinning. Because she put her trust and confidence in the Spirit and good will of God, Mary said yes to the angel who was spinning her world around. In doing that, she teaches us how to let go of our need to control and cling, just to let ourselves go in utter freedom and joy into the arms of God.

Let the primary colors of this painting remind you that it is just that simple.

Seat of Wisdom

A Lamentation

O Wisdom, O Mother,
bright spirit of Light,
rocking together,
embraced by the night.

Attend to our world,
filled with lament.
Attend to our prayers,
shaken by death.

This age lives in foolishness,
abandoning our dreams,
aborting our young,
forgetting our old.

We live blindly in lies,
in shadows and stench.
We see only in traces,
in fragments and fear.
We yearn for knowledge,
but keep missing the point.
We are made for each other,
but keep dancing alone.

We cry to you, our mother
in our confusion.
Do not abandon us, your children.

O Spirit of God,
speak truth to the Church.
Ravish our hearts
with your words from above.

O Mother of Mercy,
our sweetness and hope,
embrace all your children
and forget not your own.

O Wisdom Incarnate,
illumine our minds
and direct us to others
as the bearers of light.

O Wisdom, O Mother,
bright spirit of Light,
remember your children
embraced by the night.

O Mother of the Word Incarnate...
hear and answer us
(Memorare)

"Throne of Wisdom" is an ancient title for Mary, whose lap is literally the resting place for God incarnate. Our mother's lap is the sacred place of origin for our entire life's worth of cuddling, affection, and affirmation. For the rest of our lives, it is the place we will instinctively yearn to run to when the going gets tough, no matter how old we get or how big we grow. It is in this most honored of seats that we discover our capacity for love and our need to be loved in return. And it is here, in our mother's lap, that the secrets of holy wisdom are first whispered in our ears: hush; don't be afraid; everything will be okay; I am here. And best of all: no mother could love her child more than I love you. God is such a mother.

Usually Seat of Wisdom images depict Mary sitting majestically on a golden throne. Her son, the King of kings, sits in her lap with his hands extended to us in blessing. His baby face typically has an adult-like countenance, suggesting the worldly-wise look of a grown man.

Since most of us learn wisdom and the basic lessons of life on seats much humbler than thrones, Mary is shown here in a rocking chair. The Holy Spirit, in all her wisdom, will only meet us where we are, not where we think we are supposed to be. The Spirit uses all the ordinary people and simple events of our life stories to gently and patiently guide us toward holy wisdom, transforming ordinary rockers into thrones of extraordinary power.

Promised Land of Milk & Honey

Blessed are you, O Lord,
God of all creation.
Through your goodness,
we have been called into life
and created in your image
and likeness.

Blessed are you, O Lord,
God of heaven and earth.
In the beginning you set us
alive in a garden and
promised that we would
live in a land flowing with
milk and honey.

But we have gone astray.
We have become polluted rags,
soaked with ingratitude
for life,
stained with the decay
of our own souls.

Blessed are you, O Lord,
God of the universe,
for you did not leave us alone.
In Mary you started
a new creation.
In her, the garden has
been replanted,
flowing once more with
the riches of your life.
It blooms, it grows.
May we drink fully of your gift.
May this milk and honey
cover all the world with
wonder and praise.

Blessed are you, Lord, our God,
in our Mother Mary
and in her Son, Jesus,
who is the promise made flesh
for all to taste and see.

Amen.

That we may be made worthy of the promises of Christ

(Angelus)

Many of the ancient titles of Mary, such as this one from an Orthodox litany, spring from Hebrew Testament images of longing for the Messiah and freedom from exile and slavery. The historical figure of Mary, the devout Jewish maiden, would have been well versed in the stories of Moses and Aaron and their sister, the prophet Miriam, for whom she was named. Miriam picked up a tambourine and danced in celebration when her people made it safely through the Red Sea en route to the Promised Land, the land of milk and honey to which they would journey for forty long years.

Over the centuries, many images have been created of Mary nursing her baby. These are sometimes called Our Lady of Bon Secours, or good and holy succor or aid. Reliquaries purported to contain her milk were sources of popular devotion for pilgrims in the Middle Ages. It is a beautiful image to contemplate: God incarnate draws life from the breasts of a mere mortal and leads us to the land of long-awaited abundance as promised by the prophets for generations.

Here, milk and honey, timeless symbols of purity and sweetness, flow from the holy source, the Mother of us all.

Nourished by this grace we, too, can journey to our own promised lands, where dreams are fulfilled and broken selves made whole.

Like Miriam, we will dance in joy when we reach that place of abundance.

Mother of Sorrows

Can we talk, Mary?
Tell of your pain,
tell of your sufferings?
Can we talk, Mary?
Tell of my guilt,
tell of my shame?

Can we speak, Mother of Sorrows,
your son held close to your heart—
clutching my past, counting my fears?
Mary, hold me, too.
There was a time when all was well,
the world was good,
my heart was filled.

And then came death, a death of sorts,
stunning news, shocking loss.

Now
I stand numb.
Darkness falls.
I stand with you.

Let us hold each other, Mother.
Behold, resurrection is rumored.

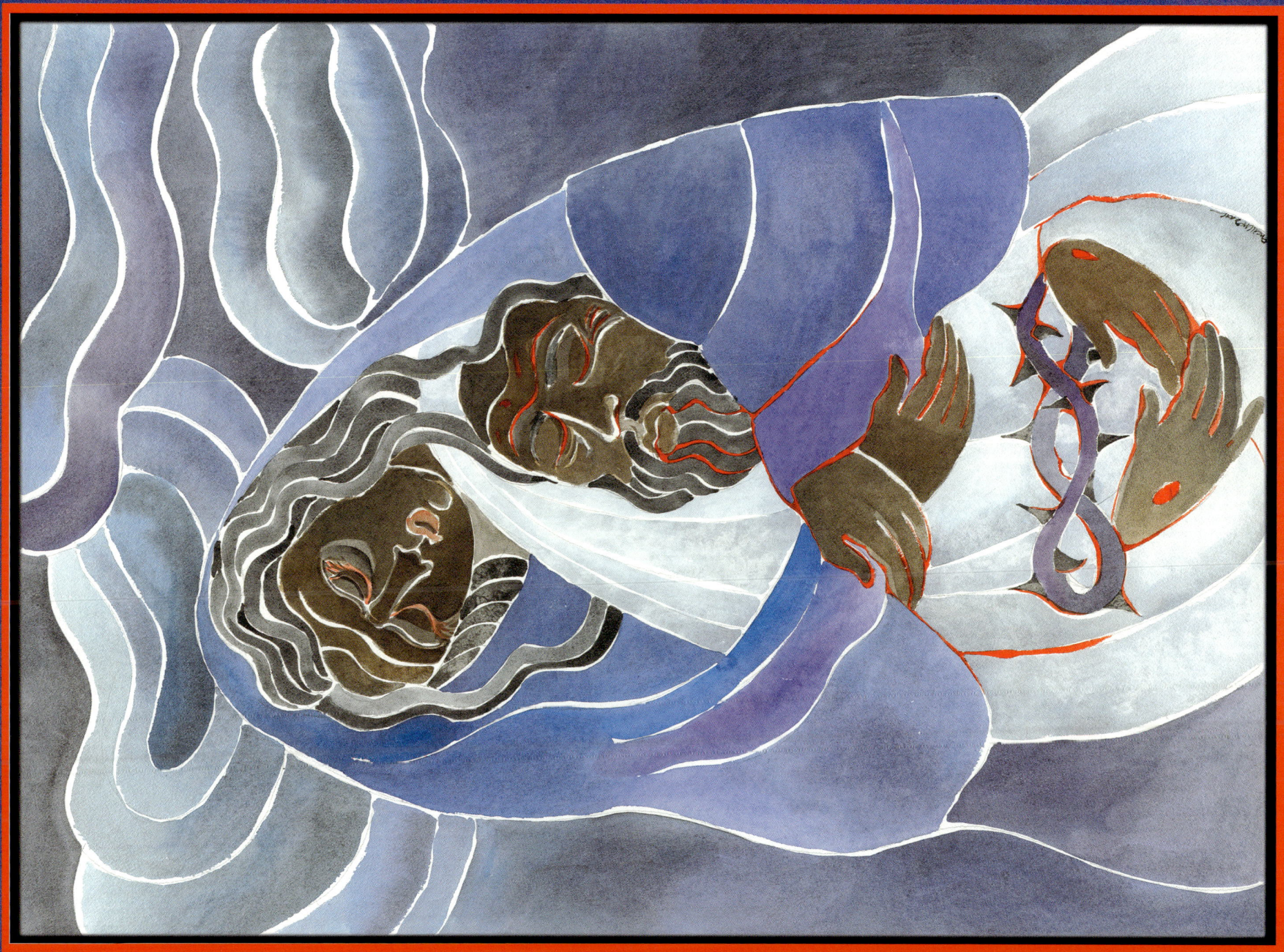

The pietà is one of the most enduring images in Christian art. It is one of Mary's seven sorrows, as foretold by Simeon at the Presentation, and the thirteenth station of the cross. It is the shadow side of the Christmas scene, when the young mother holds her baby in sublime joy as angels fill the starry sky with song. Here she holds the battered body of that same son fully grown, and leads us through the unspeakably difficult passage from the emptiness of death to the fullness of new life.

The pain of grief is a birth process into a new reality, one that we didn't ask for or choose. Long after I completed this very monochromatic image, it dawned on me that I had painted a scene of nests and wombs to symbolize this painful process. The clouds that covered the earth with darkness during the Crucifixion are womb-like shapes nesting one within the other. The bloodstained crown of thorns nests in Jesus' cupped hands. And in the most prominent nest of all, Mary cradles the egg-shaped body of her dead son.

There is good reason why the feast of Our Lady of Sorrows (September 15) falls on the day after the feast of the Holy Cross. Our Lady of Sorrows teaches us that we don't get over grief, we go through it. She hovers over us like a mother bird and holds us in our sadness. She creates a nest in the Tree of Life for our broken-hearted selves and in the right time nudges us gently forward. With newfound confidence we fly.

Mother Lady Mystic Queen

Our Lady of Peace

Remember, O most peaceful
Virgin Mary,
remember us, who cry to you
from this valley of death,
from this pit of war,
from this place of
bigotry and intolerance.

Remember us in your prayers,
dear Mother.
Bend down to break the violence,
the hatred that surrounds us.
Pray for us to your Son,
for we are locked in prisons,
the prisons of our own making—
we are sealed in tombs,
buried alive in our fears.
We are like marrowless bones,
hollow—
we have no tomorrow.

But, you, noble woman,
you hold the spirit of Christ
in your hands,
the dove of consolation,
the messenger of
a promised land.

Send forth your spirit
and grace us with
the olive branch of hope,
that we may know a world
where enemies begin to speak
to one another,
where those who are estranged
join hands in friendship,
where nations seek the way
of peace together.

Send forth your spirit,
O Queen of Peace,
and renew the face
of the earth.

Amen.

Turn . . . *your eyes of mercy toward us*
(Hail, Holy Queen)

One of the most religiously powerful experiences I've had to date was in Jerusalem, a city pulsating with the collective energies of three of the world's great religions, energies that are at once enthralling and nerve-racking. For Jews, it is the city of King David, given by God as their spiritual center and home. For Christians, it is the place where Jesus suffered, died, and rose from the dead. And for Muslims, it is the home of the great prophets to which Mohammed was transported on his night journey from Mecca and ascended into heaven.

The center point of all this spiritual frenzy is the Western Wall, the last remnant of the great Temple first built by Solomon and a great symbol of hope and lamentation. Because so many Jewish tears have been shed there, it is sometimes known as the "Wailing Wall." Young soldiers with machine guns strapped to their backs pray alongside bearded old men who look like Isaiah or Jeremiah incarnate. They bow and sway before the massive stones and leave prayers written on little slips of paper in the crevices. Jesus would have made pilgrimage every year to this temple, most famously when he was lost there at the age of twelve. And on the platform high above it all is the Muslim Dome of the Rock, which houses the rock on which Abraham was to sacrifice his son, Isaac.

Our Lady of Light

Breathe on us,
   O Spirit of Fire.
Consume us,
   O Spirit of Love.

Descend on us,
   O Spirit of Power.
Visit us,
   O Spirit of God.

Astonish us with new life
as you astonished Mary of Nazareth.

Touch our hearts with joy
as you touched Mary of Bethlehem.

Fill us with vintage wine
as you filled Mary of Cana.

Console us with each other
as you consoled Mary of Calvary.

Kindle us with your fire
as you kindled Mary of Pentecost.

May our hearts burn within us;
with Mary, may we sparkle
with the radiance of Christ.
         Amen.

To you do we cry, poor banished children of Eve
(Hail, Holy Queen)

This scene of a rainy day in the Garden of Paradise sprang out of my desire to paint with lots of gray, a color I rarely use. Like a gentle spring rain, it served to quiet my senses after painting so many brightly colored images in this series. It reminded me, in its soothing way, that gray is the color of primordial mist and sky, of balance and serenity. We need the occasional gray, wet day if we truly wish to savor the multicolored beauty of the garden.

Grace falls on us like rain and rain falls on weed and flower alike. It soaks us to the bone and drenches us with divine goodness and inspiration. We don't deserve it nor do we always ask for it. It is freely given and freely received, a shower from the Holy Spirit to liven up our dry spells.

Mary, pregnant with the source of divine grace, is a new Eve in the Garden of Paradise. Like Eve, she has been given the freedom to make choices and enter the fullness of abundant life. Unlike Eve, who hid in the bushes with Adam at the sound of God's voice, Mary stands tall in her humble response. Instead of covering herself in shame, as they did, Mary opens her arms to the rain and says, "Yes, let it be done to me as you say. Rain on me, soak me through and through." Free of our original fears and weaknesses that come with being children of Eve and Adam, Mary walks us without stumbling through the garden, drenched in the grace of God's love.

Our Lady of Divine Grace, the New Eve

Gracious Mother, New Eve,
Rain down your grace upon us.
Attune our minds and lift our hearts
Toward Christ, the Tree of Life.
Immersed in Him and He in us,
All things are bright in the garden.

Peaceful woman, New Eve of grace,
Long has the world waited.
Enough of winter! Let spring appear!
New hope, new colors encircle us,
Abandoned together to the will of God.

Ave turns Eva around, O Mary.
Virgin most holy, Mother of God,
Extend your hands; hold us in prayer.

          Amen.

Here, Mary sits in front of the wall cradling the Holy Spirit with an olive branch of peace. Their haloes create openings in the stones that give small glimpses of the wide expanse of blue heaven above and beyond the dividing walls of earth. She is dressed in black and white to suggest the complementarity of opposites, wearing a *tallis*, or Jewish prayer shawl, on one side, and a *keffiyeh*, or Palestinian scarf, on the other.

We all have walls around our hearts wherein mighty battles of fear and resentment are waged. Forces of "right" and "wrong," truth and deceit, sinfulness and saintliness wreak havoc within them. Let us be guided by the Queen of Peace to disassemble these walls, stone by stone, and open our hearts to the bright blue sky of the heavenly Jerusalem.

Rejoice and be glad, O Virgin Mary, …
for the Lord has indeed risen, alleluia
(Regina Caeli)

According to Luke, Mary was in the upper room with the disciples of Jesus on that first Pentecost day, when the Holy Spirit blew the roof off the place and descended upon them in brilliant flames of enlightenment. In this image, a small tongue of fire rests on Mary's head and ignites her entire being, spreading outward and fanned by the *ruah* (breath) of God. She holds the light of Christ close to her heart but at the same time offers it to us, inviting us to embrace our own freely given gifts of grace.

Deep within us, far beneath the surface of our skin, under our hearts and bones, behind the shadows of our egos, burns an eternal flame. I like to think of it not as the molten core at the center of the earth (because most of us couldn't live with that constant drama and intensity), but more like a pilot light—even, steady, and reliable. It pulls us gently toward itself, calling us over and over again to see ourselves in new light, to rediscover the full range of our inner gifts and potentialities.

Red is the color of passion, blood, fire, all things human. Yellow is the sun, Jesus the light, the color of glory, of all things divine. When mixed they create orange, the most exuberant and energetic of colors. Together they are Pentecost, our celebration of the infinite ways in which God illuminates the dark regions of our hearts and minds with healing grace.

Our Lady of the Rosary

Hail Mary,
accept me into your school,
full of grace.
Repeat your lessons to me,
over and over,
until I learn the way,
the truth, and the life of
your Son, Jesus, the Lord.

Hail Mary,
accept me into your school,
the Lord is with you.
Shape me with the joy of
the Word-made-flesh,
that I, too, may share in
the wonder of God.

Hail Mary,
accept me into your school,
blessed are you among women.
Walk with me in the ways of sorrow,
that I may not shrink from
the lessons of pain
and the wisdom of
suffering.

Hail Mary,
accept me into your school,
blessed is the fruit of your womb.
Reveal to me the luminous gift
of the one who
healed the sick,
raised the dead,
and shares his body and blood
with us.

Hail Mary,
accept me into your school,
now and at the hour of
my death,
that I may live forever
in the glorious presence
of God,
in the great communion
of love,
where you now live
and reign
with your Son
and the hosts of heaven
forever and ever.
Amen.

Hail Mary, full of grace, the Lord is with you
(Hail Mary)

One of the most memorable trips I've ever made was a pilgrimage to Santiago de Compostela in Spain. Starting in Paris, we followed one of the routes that have been popular among pilgrims ever since the Middle Ages. I brought with me a rosary that had belonged to my recently deceased father, and at each holy shrine and cathedral along the way, I would remove a bead and leave it in a secret place. I like to think that those rosary beads are still nestled inside pillars and behind altars throughout France and Spain.

So many religious symbols hold a mixture of fear and fascination for a child, and the rosary frightened me as a kid. The low monotonous hum of the prayers seemed like an incantation from a scary movie, and on top of that, the rosary was the first thing my mother would reach for in anxious moments. But over time I've learned that's kind of the whole point of sacred mystery, and I've replaced fear and alarm with awe and wonder. That pilgrimage, and plenty of walking since, is what has helped me make the switch. The repetitious mantra of prayers helps me enter the big mysteries of life rather than shrink in fear from them. The Joyful Mysteries celebrate God-made-flesh and the bright spots on our homebound journey. When we feel broken and lonely, the Sorrowful Mysteries remind us that one day all will be well again. The Glorious Mysteries point us to our moments of transformation and grace. And the Luminous Mysteries help us to see the "Aha!" moments of illumination and awareness of God. I find I am more welcoming of joy and sorrow, more attentive to glory and moments of enlightenment.

This painting is an homage to the sacred artists of Spain and Latin America, who often clothe their statues of Mary with elaborate jewel-studded dresses. Swatches of lace, silk, and velvet are sewn with diamonds and tiny beads of gold in meticulous detail.

This image of Our Lady of the Rosary is also a tribute of sorts to the memory of that Spanish pilgrimage. Taking apart my dad's rosary and leaving the beads everywhere, I felt connected to the countless pilgrims over the ages who had gone before me in grief and the search for something new. I was able to locate my father, my mother, and my very own self in the timeless mystery of life's passages and in the unanswerable questions asked by all people across time.

We are pilgrims forever linked like beads of prayer.

Our Lady of Refuge

Under your protecting mantle,
shelter and defend me,
my refuge and my strength.

In daylight and in darkness,
shelter me, O Mary.
In winter and in spring,
shelter me, O Mary.
In doubt and in despair,
shelter me, O Mary.
In life and in death,
shelter me, O Mary.

From the clutches of
the Evil One,
defend me, dear Mother.
From the vanity of vanities,
defend me, dear Mother.
From the fear of
surrendering all to God,
defend me, dear Mother.
From the sins of my past,
defend me, dear Mother.

When I am all alone,
be my refuge, O Mary.
When the world is
hard and cold,
be my refuge, O Mary.
When my friends betray
and deny me,
be my refuge, O Mary.
When my body is folded in pain,
be my refuge, O Mary.

At the crossroads of my life,
protect me, dear Mother.
At the moments of tough love,
protect me, dear Mother.
At the times of great success,
protect me, dear Mother.
At the hour of my death,
protect me, dear Mother.

Wrap me in your mantle,
O Mother,
and flood me with
the light of your love.

Amen.

Inspired by this confidence, we turn to you
(Memorare)

As a child who happened to grow up during the Civil Rights era, I was fascinated by stories of slavery and the Underground Railroad. Among my childhood heroes were Frederick Douglass and Harriet Ross Tubman, the remarkable woman dubbed "Moses" because she led so many slaves to freedom. After making it to the Promised Land of freedom herself the first time, she returned to the South time and time again to help hundreds of other slaves do the same.

From a recent book, *Hidden in Plain View* by Raymond G. Dobard and Jacqueline L. Tobin, I've learned that quilts probably played an important role on the Underground Railroad. Certain patterns, such as the ones we see here on Mary's dress, may have acted as secret codes or maps for slaves on the run. At her womb, for example, is "wagon wheel," which instructed the slaves that a wagon would soon be heading north. Beneath that one is the "flying geese" pattern. Slaves learned that following the geese would lead to Canada. And "crossroads," the X-shaped pattern at the bottom, led the way to Cleveland, a major crossroads in the whole underground system.

As an adult I realize that all of us are slaves to something who long to be free of the chains around our hearts. Our Lady of Refuge is the perfect "Moses" on this treacherous journey to freedom. She guides us from the cold night of winter outside her cape to the hope of eternal springtime within.

Mother   Lady   Mystic   Queen

Virgin of Virgins

Dear God,
 I am but a child, not known by man;
 how can this come to be?
What will happen, what next?
Not fully aware, I enter with veiled eyes—
  wide open—
  inside.

As bride, as daughter, as mother
 you call me.
Blessing and gift
 or curse and pain?
Perhaps a bit of each,
like roses that bloom and fade.

Yet the angels surround me.
 I hear their wings.
I find comfort and calm
 in the murmuring air.

I can only proclaim
 my joy and my thanks
 in knowing you,
 my spouse,
 my father,
 my son.

  Amen.

"How can this be, since I am a virgin?"
(Luke 1:34, NRSV)

Over the centuries, much emphasis has been placed on the physical aspects of Mary's virginity. The vocabulary around her has been full of words such as "immaculate," "spotless," "most pure," "undefiled." While there is tremendous beauty in these words and concepts, they have too often sent out the signal that to be other than virginally pure, or to celebrate one's physical and sexual self, is to cut oneself off from an intimate relationship with God. Setting the bar so impossibly high has too often led to shame and a lack of self-esteem on the part of women and cruel judgment on the part of men. And worst of all, it suggests that sexual awareness and fulfillment somehow block access to God in our hearts.

This painting is my way of seeing Mary, the Virgin of Virgins, through a different lens. Her veil suggests the hidden beauty of humility. Our most beautiful parts, the parts beneath the surface, are for God's eyes only. Her pure white dress suggests the openness to God and availability to the Holy Spirit that each of us yearns for throughout our lives. Spiritually speaking, we are virgins over and over again on the journey through life. Whenever we offer up to God our truest selves—heart, body, and soul— we set ourselves on a path through virgin territory. We enter mystery. We wonder how it can be. We discover that God makes all things possible. We say, "Let it be done to me as you say."

Mystical Rose

My dear friend,
angels crown me with flowers,
I am covered with a mantle of light.
I am called the Mystical Rose.

And yet, it is the child I bear
who is the Rose that blooms
from Jesse's stem.
He blooms mystically from me—
his fragrance purifies
the sin of the world.

In water and spirit,
you also have been crowned
and are covered in a mantle of light.
You are anointed in the fragrance
of the Holy One.

Beauty enfolds you.

So fear not:
the Rose of Salvation
will bloom again,
for you and I are one
in the mystery of love.

Bloom on.

Amen.

And the Word became flesh and made his dwelling among us

(John 1:14)

Every Advent, Christians sing a hauntingly beautiful hymn in anticipation of Jesus' birth. Inspired by metaphors from the prophet Isaiah, "Lo, How a Rose E'er Blooming" compares this monumental event to the unfolding of a simple rose, the queen of all flowers. The rose remains a pre-eminent symbol of the human soul opening to fullness in an ever-spiralling journey to the center. It is thus the perfect symbol and title for Mary, pregnant with hope and healing love.

Of the many flowers that serve as symbols for Mary, the rose is perhaps the most commonly recognized. It is the inspiration for the rosary, which began as a garland of roses. A rose with five petals brings to mind the five mysteries: red for the sorrowful, white for joyful, and yellow for glorious. Rose windows, the huge circles of stained glass dedicated to Mary, greet us as we pass through cathedral doors, leaving one world and entering another.

Roses are strong yet gentle reminders that all earthly beauty not only comes from God, it is meant to lead our hearts back to God.

As St. Francis de Sales said, "We pray best before beauty." We hold beauty close to our hearts when we discover it. We listen intently to what it has to say, we gaze in awe at what it has to show us. Beauty enlivens our senses, gives us pause, and makes us glad to be alive. The simple rose, ultimate symbol of beauty, is the perfect description of Mary, Mystical Rose.

Dawn of the Mystic Day

There is something
fresh about mornings,
dear Lady,
a sense of newness
unfolding,
a quiet promise of
the day to come.

Day breaks swiftly.
Darkness disappears
in rosy haze from
reluctant planets
in glowing azure sky.

At dawn we call upon you,
bright morning light.
You are the beginning of
a sweeping freshness
that has appeared in history,
the freshness of life
that ends death and
awakens dry bones.

O Mary, Aurora,
Dawn of the Mystic Day,
sharpen our attention
that we may be awake to
the One you announce,
the Morning Star
that never sets,
the same yesterday,
today, and tomorrow.
                    Amen.

Behold the handmaid of the Lord
(Angelus)

Things dawn upon us all the time. Sudden inspirations come to us out of the blue. Memories long forgotten come back to us with new meaning and insight. Connections are made, bridges are crossed, and we enjoy the occasional "Aha!" moment of new discovery. It feels as if finally we have found something that has been lost for too long.

This was the feeling of the prophets who lived at the time of Jesus' birth. Zechariah, the father of John the Baptist, uttered some beautifully prophetic words in a canticle still prayed today. He said that the birth of Christ was like dawn breaking upon the world, shining on all who live in darkness and the shadow of death and guiding our feet on the path to peace. When Jesus was presented in the temple by his parents, Simeon and Anna recognized him as this long-awaited light. A traditional prayer calls Mary the dawn, Christ the perfect day. And in our own time, Thomas Merton coined another poetic image of dawn when he called it "virgin time," the moment when the deep darkness of night gives way to sunlight.

This painting is filled with the pink and lavender colors of dawn, my favorite time of day. Looking out my east-facing window, coffee in hand, I am able to watch the still-hushed world spring gradually to life and welcome the dreams and inspirations that filled my head during the night. Some of these stick around into the day and become working ideas, while others get lost on what I have come to think of as the world's biggest back burner, that place where I live so much of my life. Every dawn is gift and promise and all we have to do is show up for it.

Gate of Heaven

My dear child:
Arise. Come in, please.
The gates of heaven
are opened for you.
Behold, the winter is over,
your days of mourning
are past.
Behold, my Son who died
is now alive anew;
in him
death has been slain
and life is victorious.
So enter, dear child.
I point the way for you.
Receive the inheritance
prepared for you
from the beginning
of time.

My dear Mother:
This is too much to believe,
beyond my wildest dreams.
Can this be real—
that the gift of your Son
is given so freely to me?

I am only emerging
from the darkness,
from the chrysalis,
a butterfly unfolding
its wings,
feeling its way.
O Mother, enter with me.
Show me the way.
Bind me to your Son
that I may never leave
this holy place of peace.
I stumble now;
let me lean on you
as we cross the threshold.

My dear child:
Take my hand.
My Son is the gate.
Enter with me.
Lift up your head
and behold the presence
of God.
Listen!
Oh, how the birds
are singing!

*After this our exile
show us the blessed fruit
of your womb, Jesus*

(Hail, Holy Queen)

For several years I had a studio in a classroom of a vacant Catholic school building. Just opening the door every morning when I arrived became a prayer because I was literally opening a door to a world of creativity and meditation. And to make matters even better, less than a mile from that studio was the cemetery where my parents are buried. Every day I would drive through the wrought iron gates, park my car at their row, say a quick hello, and proceed to take my daily walk. It is a beautiful old cemetery with meandering tree-lined pathways and ornately carved headstones and mausoleums. I became familiar with all the family names and stone angels and saints and used them as landmarks. Turn left at the O'Briens, turn right at the Pietà.

Both places were sacred ground, and both places had doors or gates as entryways. Gateways and doors hold lots of spiritual significance for us. With every new chapter in our lives, every addition and loss, every love and heartbreak, we cross another threshold of self-awareness and spiritual enlightenment. And each of these crossings reminds us of the ultimate one we will one day make. This is what Gate of Heaven is all about.

Mary is the Gate of Heaven because through her, Jesus passed from heaven to earth—the opposite of what we do! I went a little crazy with pearls here because they are symbols of pure beauty that are created from an irritation for the poor oyster. The curious detail of Jesus holding a butterfly on a leash was inspired by a fifteenth-century painting by Gentile da Fabriano in the National Gallery. As a symbol of the Resurrection, it reminds us of what awaits us on the other side of those pearly gates.

Star of the Sea

The birds, Mary—
the ones in the portrait—
they're gliding,
not tossed
by the storms
and the waves.
Let us be so, Mary—
free to fly,
not tossed about.

The blue, Mary—
chosen with an artist's eye,
a blue of darkness,
a blue of night.
Yet there is light
and the sun dances
in the water.
Darkness is dark no longer.
Let us be so, Mary—
filled with light,
even in darkness.

The tension, Mary—
the way the lines move,
at once so turbulent
and so peaceful.
Let us be so, Mary—
calm in the
eye of the storm.

In all that is noticed,
a song comes to heart
and swells up within me.
How can I keep from singing
the wonder and
the praises of God?
Amen.

To thee do we cry . . .
to thee do we send up our sighs
(Hail, Holy Queen)

My favorite of all the Black Madonnas I have come upon is in Rocamadour, a cliff town in France. She is a small, crudely carved figure wearing a crown and holding the child Jesus in her lap. The most dramatic feature of all in a town built on dramatic features are the model ships suspended from the ceiling, hung there by grateful sailors who survived terrible storms at sea after praying to the Virgin of Rocamadour for protection. In addition, hundreds of notes and plaques inscribed with the simple word *merci* cover the wall, left there by grateful pilgrims who, through Mary's intercession, survived storms of many other kinds.

In two separate titles Mary has been given the title of star. As the Morning Star, she is the first star in the sky, a shining symbol that the long, dark night will soon be over when the sun, the Light of the World, appears. As Star of the Sea, or Stella Maris, she is a shimmering beacon of hope and confidence when the darkness seems too deep and the ocean too wide.

In this painting, Mary rises up like a tower of light from the ocean depths. Resting on her head is a six-pointed star, the number and shape of wholeness and completion. Amid churning waters she holds her cape wide open to reveal another world, an ocean of clear, calm serenity where birds fly in freedom toward the light. Under her protection, rivers of stress and turmoil become streams of rest and delight.

Mother Lady Mystic Queen

Queen of the Apostles

O Queen of Apostles,
you were sent by God
to bear Christ
to the world.

You are sovereign of all
who have been sent out
through the ages.

We acknowledge you,
O gracious one.
You are sovereign
because you were first
to be sent out
to give birth to
the Divine Word,
the Word
that lights up the way,
the Word
who is the beacon
of clarity
in this obscure time
of broken promises
and shattered dreams.

Inspiration of your
Son's first apostles,
now inspire us in
the apostolic way.

Encourage our weak hearts
and drooping spirits
with your motherly gaze
so that we may also
be sent out
to witness to Christ,
giving birth to Jesus
in our lives.

May the net of
God's compassion and mercy
catch the heart and imagination
of everyone who
encounters us.

Amen.

Never was it known that anyone who . . . implored your help . . . was left unaided

(Memorare)

Inside every human heart is an ocean teeming with the light and life of God. It is filled with our most heartfelt prayers and soulful yearnings. It holds our dreams of glory and visions of better days to come. It is a deep world of symbols, images, and memories all wrapped up in the details of our life stories. It is where we encounter the Savior who calls us forth in faith to go out and spread the Good News, just as he did with the first apostles.

This painting is about the missionary fervor we feel when we dive into this ocean within. We have no other choice or desire than to share the story of what we see there. The first apostles went to the far corners of the known world to preach the Word. According to the stories of the early church, Mary Magdalene, the apostle to the apostles, went to France, where she lived her days as an itinerant preacher. James took his message to Spain and Thomas headed for India. Following their lead, missionaries have been circling the globe with the same message ever since.

Each of us is called to be an apostle, to cross our own seas and witness to the Word as we come to know it. It is a daunting mission, but the Queen of the Apostles will rise from the depths as a harbor of safety in the midst of this sometimes turbulent passage. With the Word as the mast of our ship, and guided by the wind of the Holy Spirit, our nets will teem with miraculous abundance and we will return safely home.

Queen of the Angels

We would make music
in your chambers,
O Queen of Angels,
with strings and reeds,
with trumpets and drums.

We would join
our mortal talents
in a symphony of
praise to you,
with seraphim and cherubim,
with angels and archangels,
with virtues, principalities,
and powers.

But we stand mute,
our instruments silent,
O Queen,
dark with pain,
straining at glory.

O Queen,
single mother,
widowed wife,
O Queen,
refugee woman,
slain at the cross;
You know our suffering,
O Queen of the
Heavenly Host.

Send us the angels.
Let them visit our earth
torn by war,
raped by greed,
battered by fear.

Send us the angels,
O Queen,
to teach us to
make music with them
that will please
your ears
and give glory to
God in the highest.

The angel of the Lord declared unto Mary

(Angelus)

This title conjures up so many images in my mind's eye. I can see armies of angels surrounding Mary like a fortress or a wide circle of angels buzzing around her like bees around a flower. What came out of me first, however, was this image of a jazz band of angelic musicians accompanying Mary as she sings her Magnificat. Banjo, horn, and drums belt out the praises of God, turning the smoke of a nightclub into the incense of a cathedral.

Music is one of the greatest gifts for healing that we humans have. It is therapy for the dying and balm for the heartsick. It soothes us into serenity when the world is too noisy and gets our feet jumping when we need to dance. Music and angels surround us at all times. That blind musician on the street corner who plays the blues for your loose change may just be an archangel telling you to hang in there in the midst of your stresses. That church cantor whose heart and intentions are much bigger than her voice may be Gabriel with an important message: we are being overshadowed by a Holy Spirit with whom anything is possible.

With love towering so high in our very midst we have no choice but to add our timid voices to the heavenly chorus. In showers and choir lofts around the world, we belt out our Kyries and Alleluias. And remember this: it was angels who told the women at the tomb that first Easter morning that Jesus was long gone. Perhaps they did it with a song that they sing for us still.

Queen of the Prophets

Mysterious as the moon,
deep as the sky—
turn inward, dear Prophet.
Tell of the heart of God.

Sparkling as the stars,
elusive as the clouds—
enter the secret chambers
and speak to us of the
contours of hope.

Dark as the night,
clear as the rain—
search out for us the way
to the sun, to the center,
to the whole, to the light.

O Prophet Queen,
speak the Word afresh among us,
That the rough ways be made smooth,
that the mountains be made low,
that the world be turned around,
that the ancient oracles
come to pass.
Amen.

All generations shall call me blessed
(Magnificat)

This image is for all who are anxious about the future, who tremble in a world constantly threatened by terror and war. The Queen of the Prophets comes especially to those who struggle to live life fully in the present moment with a sense of security and hope in the age to come. She reminds us that God is on their side.

Prophets speak in the daylight of what they hear in the darkness. They go to places deep within themselves to discover the words and inspiration of the Holy Spirit. Their once shaky voices well up with confidence when they speak the words of God, just as Mary's did when she proclaimed in the Magnificat that all generations would call her blessed. Through her son, the lowly would be lifted up, the hungry would be fed.

and the promise made to Abraham and Sarah and all their children, as numerous as the stars, would at long last be fulfilled.

The moon has long been Mary's symbol because it is universally associated with the light of feminine wisdom and intuition. We might be more accustomed to images of Mary standing on the crescent moon, but here it has become her halo. It rises behind her head, filling the night sky and illuminating the darkness. Its reflected light bathes the world in a glow of silver and casts the brilliant blue shadows of divine mystery. Rising up from within Mary is the sun, the very center of her being, sheltered by her praying hands, which point upward like a Gothic cathedral. She has made a tent for the sun.

Queen of the Saints

Ave, Regina Caelorum!
Hail, Queen of the
heavenly courts,
surrounded by the
angels and the saints.
Hail, so graced by God
in holiness beyond compare.
Hail, woman of honor and
divine favor.

Ave, Domina Angelorum!
Hail, Mary, clothed with
the sun and the moon,
crowned with stars,
bearing a Son
for all to embrace.

Salve Radix! Salve Porta!
We salute you, O Mother,
root of all holy living.
We salute you,
doorway to the divine.
We join the heavenly chorus
of honor and incantation:

Abraham and Sarah salute you,
Moses and the law give you honor.
Joseph, your husband, honors you.
The Magdalen and the Little Flower
celebrate you.
Agnes and Paul extol you.
Kateri and Brigid sing your praises.
Thea Bowman and Andrew Kim
tell of your wonders.
Francis de Sales and Fra Angelico
weave words and images
to crown you.

Ex qua mundo lux est orta—
The whole church
honors you as Queen of
Matriarchs and Patriarchs.
We acclaim you as our model
of discipleship.
From you light has been
born into the world.
May we be ever grateful
for this gift.
Amen.

According to his promise...
to Abraham and to his descendants forever

(Luke 1:55)

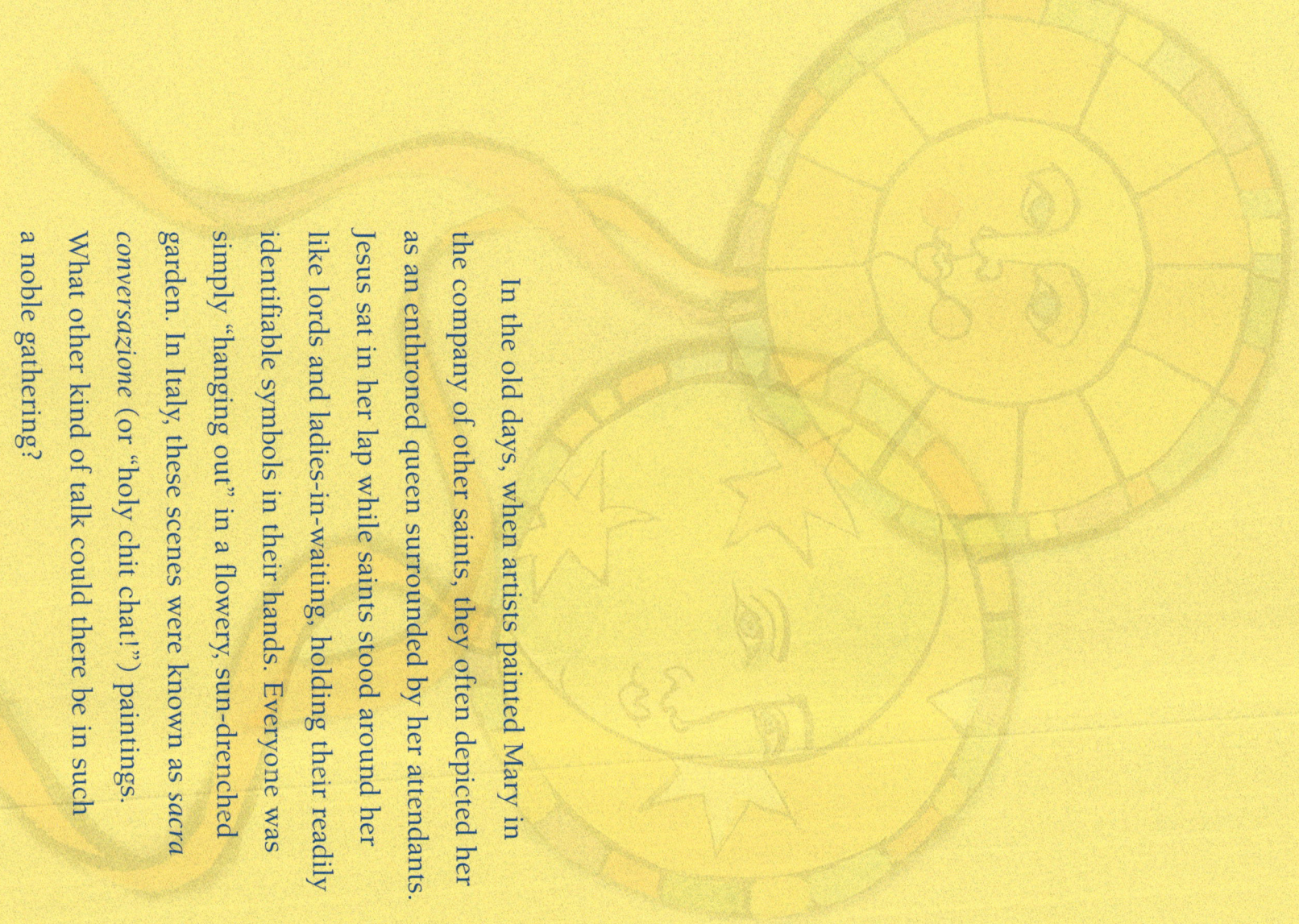

In the old days, when artists painted Mary in the company of other saints, they often depicted her as an enthroned queen surrounded by her attendants. Jesus sat in her lap while saints stood around her like lords and ladies-in-waiting, holding their readily identifiable symbols in their hands. Everyone was simply "hanging out" in a flowery, sun-drenched garden. In Italy, these scenes were known as *sacra conversazione* (or "holy chit chat!") paintings. What other kind of talk could there be in such a noble gathering?

In this painting, two balloons with flowing streamers rise above the heads of heaven's finest, emphasizing the festive atmosphere of paradise. The sun and moon faces on these balloons symbolize the timelessness of this beautiful vision. Through all ages and across the centuries, saints go marching in to bask in the company of a queen mother and her eternally holy child. Matriarchs and patriarchs, apostles and martyrs, all of them at one time, like us, broken and sinful, living now and forever in the reflected glow of the light of God. They and their queen and her child remind us that we who believe are all children of that same light.

Who are the saints and holy ones depicted here? If you know your art symbols, you won't need to read the following list of saints in the sacred conversation. On the left side, starting at the top, are Saints Mary Magdalene, Brigid of Ireland, Agnes and Paul, Blessed Fra Angelico and Kateri Tekakwitha, and Moses. On the right side are St. Joseph, the late Sr. Thea Bowman, Saints Francis de Sales, Thérèse of Lisieux, Andrew Kim, and Abraham and Sarah. At the bottom, two angels provide the musical accompaniment.

Queen of the Universe

Dear Creator of all,
We thought the earth was flat—
 we were wrong.
We thought the earth was center,
 celestial bodies circling round—
 we were wrong.
We thought we understood it all—
 we were wrong.

Dear God, we praise you!
Now we know the universe is vast,
 beyond our imagining—
 galaxies, black holes,
 supernovas, the unpredictable
 possibilities of space.

Dear God, we bless you!
At the center of all powers,
 you have placed your Christ,
 Alpha, Omega, Lord of all,
 whose Spirit fills the cosmos,
 an ocean of scintillating light.

Dear God, we thank you!
At Christ's right hand
 stands the Queen,
 arrayed in gold,
 the gold of Ophir,
 in the place of honor,
 in elegant beauty,
 crowned with the stars,
 while the angels sing.

Dear God, we stand in awe!
We gaze in wonder
 at the shining delight
 of the cosmos you create
 and re-create
 out of chaos,
 in the outrageous
 playfulness of
 your love.

Deo gratias!

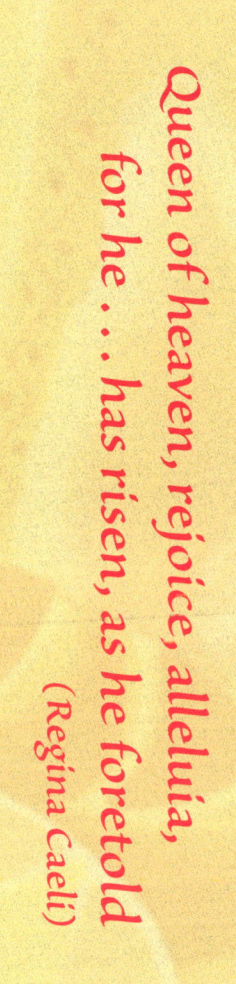

Queen of heaven, rejoice, alleluia, for he... has risen, as he foretold
(Regina Caeli)

The world gets smaller and smaller in this age of ever-changing technology and communication. At the same time, the universe around us seems to expand in its incomprehensible vastness. The more we learn of the cosmos, the more we learn how little we know. We are fifteen-minute specks in the endlessness of time and space. This realization can be as daunting as the technology is exciting.

Side by side with the thrill of new advances that make our lives longer, fuller, and healthier are the same old acts of violence that have been with us since the world began. We still send young people to war in the name of God. We gasp in horror as our towers tumble and turn to dust. And we still shake our heads in disbelief at stories of mass genocide and torture in every age around the globe. The cliché still rings true—the more we change, the more we stay the same.

Saint John knew this when he wrote in the book of Revelation about the woman clothed with the sun. For all eternity, this Queen is about to give birth to light and peace while the snarling red serpent spends that same eternity ready to devour all that is good and holy. Weeds still grow alongside wheat. Roses still have thorns. And forever singing in the far reaches of our globally warmed garden paradise is the poor young Virgin of Nazareth who became the starry-eyed mother of Bethlehem and grew into the tear-streaked matron of Calvary and the wisdom figure of Ephesus. She is queen of it all, the enormous universe extending way beyond our meager comprehension as well as the tiny universe within us, the one made ever larger by love.

Queen of Heaven, rejoice!
The Son whom you merited to bear
has risen as he said!
Pray for us and be glad!

Alleluia!

Michael O'Neill McGrath, a brother of the Oblates of St. Francis de Sales, is the author and illustrator of *Journey with Thérèse of Lisieux: Celebrating the Artist in Us All* as well as *Patrons and Protectors*, a three-part series of books on the saints. He has been the recipient of awards from the Catholic Press Association for his covers of America magazine, and his work appears regularly in the publications of today's leading Catholic and Christian publishers. Mickey is also a widely respected speaker and retreat director at parishes and retreat centers throughout the United States.

JEAN CLOUGH

KRISTINE WOLFF

Richard N. Fragomeni, a priest of the diocese of Albany, New York, is associate professor of liturgy and homiletics and chair of the Department of Word and Worship at Catholic Theological Union in Chicago. He has written widely on topics of liturgy, music, symbolism, the catechumenate, the Eucharist, and liturgies with children, among other subjects. In addition to his teaching, preaching, and writing duties, Father Fragomeni serves as spiritual director at the Shrine of Our Lady of Pompeii, an Italian-American spiritual center in Chicago's Little Italy.